THE JOB DONE RIGHT

MONTHLY BILL TRACKER BOOK!

Activinotes

Activinotes

DAILY JOURNALS, PLANNERS, NOTEBOOKS AND OTHER BLANK BOOKS

Copyright 2016

This Book Belongs To

_____

JANUARY

MONTHLY CHECKLIST

- ○ _____
- ○ _____
- ○ _____
- ○ _____
- ○ _____
- ○ _____
- ○ _____
- ○ _____
- ○ _____
- ○ _____
- ○ _____
- ○ _____
- ○ _____
- ○ _____
- ○ _____
- ○ _____

MONTHLY CHECKLIST

- ○ _____
- ○ _____
- ○ _____
- ○ _____
- ○ _____
- ○ _____
- ○ _____
- ○ _____
- ○ _____
- ○ _____
- ○ _____
- ○ _____
- ○ _____
- ○ _____
- ○ _____
- ○ _____

MONTHLY BILLS

BILL	DUE DATE	PAID	AMOUNT

MONTHLY BILLS

BILL	DUE DATE	PAID	AMOUNT

EXPENSE / BILL	AMOUNT	DUE DATE	BALANCE	PAID

MONTHLY BILL PAYMENT LOG

SAVINGS	BALANCE

EXPENSE / BILL	AMOUNT	DUE DATE	BALANCE	PAID

MONTHLY BILL PAYMENT LOG

SAVINGS	BALANCE

FEBRUARY

MONTHLY CHECKLIST

MONTHLY CHECKLIST

MONTHLY BILLS

BILL	DUE DATE	PAID	AMOUNT

MONTHLY BILLS

BILL	DUE DATE	PAID	AMOUNT

EXPENSE / BILL	AMOUNT	DUE DATE	BALANCE	PAID

MONTHLY BILL PAYMENT LOG

SAVINGS	BALANCE

EXPENSE / BILL	AMOUNT	DUE DATE	BALANCE	PAID

MONTHLY BILL PAYMENT LOG

SAVINGS	BALANCE

MARCH

MONTHLY CHECKLIST

MONTHLY CHECKLIST

- ○ _____
- ○ _____
- ○ _____
- ○ _____
- ○ _____
- ○ _____
- ○ _____
- ○ _____
- ○ _____
- ○ _____
- ○ _____
- ○ _____
- ○ _____
- ○ _____
- ○ _____
- ○ _____
- ○ _____

MONTHLY BILLS

BILL	DUE DATE	PAID	AMOUNT

MONTHLY BILLS

BILL	DUE DATE	PAID	AMOUNT

EXPENSE / BILL	AMOUNT	DUE DATE	BALANCE	PAID

MONTHLY BILL PAYMENT LOG

SAVINGS	BALANCE

EXPENSE / BILL	AMOUNT	DUE DATE	BALANCE	PAID

MONTHLY BILL PAYMENT LOG

SAVINGS	BALANCE

APRIL

MONTHLY CHECKLIST

- ○ _____
- ○ _____
- ○ _____
- ○ _____
- ○ _____
- ○ _____
- ○ _____
- ○ _____
- ○ _____
- ○ _____
- ○ _____
- ○ _____
- ○ _____
- ○ _____
- ○ _____
- ○ _____

MONTHLY CHECKLIST

- ○ _____
- ○ _____
- ○ _____
- ○ _____
- ○ _____
- ○ _____
- ○ _____
- ○ _____
- ○ _____
- ○ _____
- ○ _____
- ○ _____
- ○ _____
- ○ _____
- ○ _____
- ○ _____

MONTHLY BILLS

BILL	DUE DATE	PAID	AMOUNT

MONTHLY BILLS

BILL	DUE DATE	PAID	AMOUNT

EXPENSE / BILL	AMOUNT	DUE DATE	BALANCE	PAID

MONTHLY BILL PAYMENT LOG

SAVINGS	BALANCE

EXPENSE / BILL	AMOUNT	DUE DATE	BALANCE	PAID

MONTHLY BILL PAYMENT LOG

SAVINGS	BALANCE

МАУ

MONTHLY CHECKLIST

○ _____

○ _____

○ _____

○ _____

○ _____

○ _____

○ _____

○ _____

○ _____

○ _____

○ _____

○ _____

○ _____

○ _____

○ _____

○ _____

MONTHLY CHECKLIST

- ○ _____
- ○ _____
- ○ _____
- ○ _____
- ○ _____
- ○ _____
- ○ _____
- ○ _____
- ○ _____
- ○ _____
- ○ _____
- ○ _____
- ○ _____
- ○ _____
- ○ _____
- ○ _____

MONTHLY BILLS

BILL	DUE DATE	PAID	AMOUNT

MONTHLY BILLS

BILL	DUE DATE	PAID	AMOUNT

EXPENSE / BILL	AMOUNT	DUE DATE	BALANCE	PAID

MONTHLY BILL PAYMENT LOG

SAVINGS	BALANCE

EXPENSE / BILL	AMOUNT	DUE DATE	BALANCE	PAID

MONTHLY BILL PAYMENT LOG

SAVINGS	BALANCE

JUNE

MONTHLY CHECKLIST

- ○ _____
- ○ _____
- ○ _____
- ○ _____
- ○ _____
- ○ _____
- ○ _____
- ○ _____
- ○ _____
- ○ _____
- ○ _____
- ○ _____
- ○ _____
- ○ _____
- ○ _____
- ○ _____
- ○ _____

MONTHLY CHECKLIST

MONTHLY BILLS

BILL	DUE DATE	PAID	AMOUNT

MONTHLY BILLS

BILL	DUE DATE	PAID	AMOUNT

EXPENSE / BILL	AMOUNT	DUE DATE	BALANCE	PAID

MONTHLY BILL PAYMENT LOG

SAVINGS	BALANCE

EXPENSE / BILL	AMOUNT	DUE DATE	BALANCE	PAID

MONTHLY BILL PAYMENT LOG

SAVINGS	BALANCE

JULY

MONTHLY CHECKLIST

- ○ _____
- ○ _____
- ○ _____
- ○ _____
- ○ _____
- ○ _____
- ○ _____
- ○ _____
- ○ _____
- ○ _____
- ○ _____
- ○ _____
- ○ _____
- ○ _____
- ○ _____
- ○ _____

MONTHLY CHECKLIST

- ○ _____
- ○ _____
- ○ _____
- ○ _____
- ○ _____
- ○ _____
- ○ _____
- ○ _____
- ○ _____
- ○ _____
- ○ _____
- ○ _____
- ○ _____
- ○ _____
- ○ _____
- ○ _____

MONTHLY BILLS

BILL	DUE DATE	PAID	AMOUNT

MONTHLY BILLS

BILL	DUE DATE	PAID	AMOUNT

EXPENSE / BILL	AMOUNT	DUE DATE	BALANCE	PAID

MONTHLY BILL PAYMENT LOG

SAVINGS	BALANCE

EXPENSE / BILL	AMOUNT	DUE DATE	BALANCE	PAID

MONTHLY BILL PAYMENT LOG

SAVINGS	BALANCE

AUGUST

MONTHLY CHECKLIST

○ _____
○ _____
○ _____
○ _____
○ _____
○ _____
○ _____
○ _____
○ _____
○ _____
○ _____
○ _____
○ _____
○ _____
○ _____
○ _____

MONTHLY CHECKLIST

○ _____

○ _____

○ _____

○ _____

○ _____

○ _____

○ _____

○ _____

○ _____

○ _____

○ _____

○ _____

○ _____

○ _____

○ _____

○ _____

○ _____

MONTHLY BILLS

BILL	DUE DATE	PAID	AMOUNT

MONTHLY BILLS

BILL	DUE DATE	PAID	AMOUNT

EXPENSE / BILL	AMOUNT	DUE DATE	BALANCE	PAID

MONTHLY BILL PAYMENT LOG

SAVINGS	BALANCE

EXPENSE / BILL	AMOUNT	DUE DATE	BALANCE	PAID

MONTHLY BILL PAYMENT LOG

SAVINGS	BALANCE

SEPTEMBER

MONTHLY CHECKLIST

MONTHLY CHECKLIST

- ○ _____
- ○ _____
- ○ _____
- ○ _____
- ○ _____
- ○ _____
- ○ _____
- ○ _____
- ○ _____
- ○ _____
- ○ _____
- ○ _____
- ○ _____
- ○ _____
- ○ _____

MONTHLY BILLS

BILL	DUE DATE	PAID	AMOUNT

MONTHLY BILLS

BILL	DUE DATE	PAID	AMOUNT

EXPENSE / BILL	AMOUNT	DUE DATE	BALANCE	PAID

MONTHLY BILL PAYMENT LOG

SAVINGS	BALANCE

EXPENSE / BILL	AMOUNT	DUE DATE	BALANCE	PAID

MONTHLY BILL PAYMENT LOG

SAVINGS	BALANCE

OCTOBER

MONTHLY CHECKLIST

○ _____

○ _____

○ _____

○ _____

○ _____

○ _____

○ _____

○ _____

○ _____

○ _____

○ _____

○ _____

○ _____

○ _____

○ _____

○ _____

MONTHLY CHECKLIST

- ○ _____
- ○ _____
- ○ _____
- ○ _____
- ○ _____
- ○ _____
- ○ _____
- ○ _____
- ○ _____
- ○ _____
- ○ _____
- ○ _____
- ○ _____
- ○ _____
- ○ _____
- ○ _____
- ○ _____

MONTHLY BILLS

BILL	DUE DATE	PAID	AMOUNT

MONTHLY BILLS

BILL	DUE DATE	PAID	AMOUNT

EXPENSE / BILL	AMOUNT	DUE DATE	BALANCE	PAID

MONTHLY BILL PAYMENT LOG

SAVINGS	BALANCE

EXPENSE / BILL	AMOUNT	DUE DATE	BALANCE	PAID

MONTHLY BILL PAYMENT LOG

SAVINGS	BALANCE

NOVEMBER

MONTHLY CHECKLIST

MONTHLY CHECKLIST

- ○ _____
- ○ _____
- ○ _____
- ○ _____
- ○ _____
- ○ _____
- ○ _____
- ○ _____
- ○ _____
- ○ _____
- ○ _____
- ○ _____
- ○ _____
- ○ _____
- ○ _____
- ○ _____
- ○ _____

MONTHLY BILLS

BILL	DUE DATE	PAID	AMOUNT

MONTHLY BILLS

BILL	DUE DATE	PAID	AMOUNT

EXPENSE / BILL	AMOUNT	DUE DATE	BALANCE	PAID

MONTHLY BILL PAYMENT LOG

SAVINGS	BALANCE

EXPENSE / BILL	AMOUNT	DUE DATE	BALANCE	PAID

MONTHLY BILL PAYMENT LOG

SAVINGS	BALANCE

DECEMBER

MONTHLY CHECKLIST

- ○ _____
- ○ _____
- ○ _____
- ○ _____
- ○ _____
- ○ _____
- ○ _____
- ○ _____
- ○ _____
- ○ _____
- ○ _____
- ○ _____
- ○ _____
- ○ _____
- ○ _____
- ○ _____

MONTHLY CHECKLIST

- ◯ _____
- ◯ _____
- ◯ _____
- ◯ _____
- ◯ _____
- ◯ _____
- ◯ _____
- ◯ _____
- ◯ _____
- ◯ _____
- ◯ _____
- ◯ _____
- ◯ _____
- ◯ _____
- ◯ _____
- ◯ _____
- ◯ _____

MONTHLY BILLS

BILL	DUE DATE	PAID	AMOUNT

MONTHLY BILLS

BILL	DUE DATE	PAID	AMOUNT

EXPENSE / BILL	AMOUNT	DUE DATE	BALANCE	PAID

MONTHLY BILL PAYMENT LOG

SAVINGS	BALANCE

EXPENSE / BILL	AMOUNT	DUE DATE	BALANCE	PAID

MONTHLY BILL PAYMENT LOG

SAVINGS	BALANCE